Beloved Memories Of

....

A Faithful Friend.